SAVED!
NOW
WHAT?

A 20 Day Devotional
for Kids

BY BETSY ADAMS

ILLUSTRATED BY CATHY HALL

FOUR:14
PUBLISHING
FORNEY, TEXAS

Text and Illustrations copyright © 2020 Betsy Adams
Published by Four Fourteen Publishing

Hardback ISBN-13: 978-1-7349650-2-5
Paperback ISBN-13: 978-1-7349650-1-8
eBook ISBN-13: 978-1-7349650-0-1

Library of Congress Control Number: 2020941657

Cover design by 100Covers
Interior design by FormattedBooks

DEDICATION

Author Dedication
To my husband, Keith, for his constant support of my dreams.
To Blake, Stephanie, Brooke, and Morgan, for raising good humans.
To my grandchildren, for their constant inspiration.

Illustrator Dedication
To my husband, whom I love and cherish. Thank you for
choosing me. You spread gentleness and faithfulness!
To my children and grandchildren, whom I love.
My son, who always makes me laugh and keeps a smile on his face. You spread joy!
My daughter, who is always selfless and encouraging. You spread love!
My son-in-law, who is always helpful. You spread kindness!
To my daughter-in-law, who is always level-headed and caring. You spread hope!
To my WeeOnes, who are hilarities. I pray that one day you will claim Christ
as your Savior and follow Him all the days of your lives. Spread Jesus!

NOTE TO PARENTS

O nce children accept Christ as their Lord and Savior, it is so important to help them understand the next steps. Living a life for Christ is about how we love God and love others. It's about our behavior and how we interact with the people around us. It's important for children to understand that what we think about and how we act are direct reflections of our relationship with God.

The devotion for each day includes a few statements, a verse relating to those statements, and an application piece. Suggestions are given for something to talk about, something to write about, and something to do. Children can use a journal or record their ideas directly in the book by writing or drawing pictures. Pick and choose what works best for you and your family.

Numbers 6:24-26
NIV

The Lord bless you and keep you; the Lord make His face shine on you and be gracious to you; the Lord turn His face toward you and give you peace.

INTRODUCTION
SAVED† NOW WHAT?

You have accepted Jesus Christ as your Lord and Savior, and are now a child of the King! This means you have an amazing inheritance for all of eternity. Although that is hard to understand now, it is important to know your decision is only the beginning. I know without a doubt that we, as Christians, will be in Heaven together some day. But before any of us reach Heaven, we have important work to do here. We want others to know about God, and that is best shared through the way we talk, the way we act, and how we spend our time.

What we think about affects how we live. How we fill our mind matters. In 2 Corinthians 10:5, the Bible says, "Capture every thought and make it give up and obey Christ" (ICB). This means if we are worried about something, or have mean thoughts about someone, we can give that thought away—give it up. Then we think about the good things in our lives, the good things God has done for us, like sending His Son to die on the cross so we can be forgiven and have everlasting life (John 3:16)!

Philippians 4:8 (NIV) helps us know what to think about. It's a good starting place.

Finally, brothers and sisters, whatever is true, whatever is right, whatever is pure, whatever is lovely, whatever is admirable—if anything is excellent or praiseworthy—think on such things.

I believe God wants us to fill our minds with good things, so kind words and actions come out in our behavior. Remember, it is how we respond with our words and our actions that shows others that we love God.

1

DAY 1

Whatever is True

Whatever is true, think about such things. This means to be genuine, loyal, and truthful. When you say you are sorry, you need to really mean it. When you say you are going to help someone or do your chores, you need to really do it. It's important to think about how your actions and words affect others.

God wants us to be thoughtful. Our words should be helpful, not harmful. Our words should build trust.

Proverbs 3:3
ICB

Don't ever stop being kind and truthful. Let kindness and truth show in all you do. Write them down in your mind as if on a tablet.

💬 Something to talk about:

Can you think of a time when you apologized to someone because you were really sorry (and not because your mom made you)?

✏️ Something to write about:

Why do you think it is important to be truthful?

_____

_____

_____

_____

_____

_____

_____

_____

_____

☑️ Something to do:

Work hard this week to be positive. Try not to whine or complain.

DAY 2

Whatever is Honorable

Whatever is honorable, think about such things. This means to have a good reputation or a good name. It means people think well of you or have good thoughts about you and your actions. Qualities like working hard, being kind, and doing what is right help give you a good name. Following the rules, playing fair, and being truthful shows people they can depend on you.

We can depend on God for everything we need. When we trust God to take care of us, we are more confident to step out and help others.

Titus 3:2
The Message

...always ready to lend a helping hand. No insults, no fights.
God's people should be bighearted and courteous.

💬 Something to talk about:

Can you think of a time you were dependable/honorable?

✏️ Something to write about:

What can you do to develop a good name, an honorable name?

_____

_____

_____

_____

_____

_____

_____

_____

_____

_____

☑️ Something to do:

Look for ways to help someone this week.

DAY 3

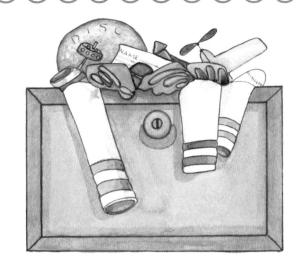

Whatever is Right

Whatever is right, think about such things. This word is easy to *talk* about. It is simply doing what is right, which *isn't* always easy. When you think about doing what is right, you probably think of things like obeying your mom and dad, cleaning your room, or listening to your teachers. You know when something is right or wrong. You know if your actions will help someone or hurt someone. It is important to think about things that help others, and to think about the right things to do.

God is happy when we do the right thing, especially when it's hard.

Psalm 15:2
The Message

Walk straight, act right, tell the truth.

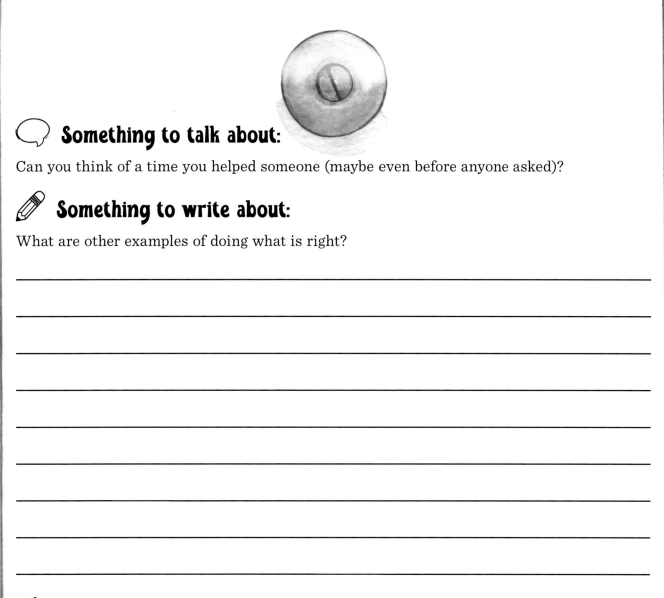

💬 Something to talk about:

Can you think of a time you helped someone (maybe even before anyone asked)?

✏️ Something to write about:

What are other examples of doing what is right?

_____

_____

_____

_____

_____

_____

_____

_____

☑️ Something to do:

Do your chores this week without being asked by your mom or dad.

DAY 4

Whatever is Pure

Whatever is pure, think about such things. Every day you have choices about what you watch, what you listen to, and what you think about. *Whatever is pure* is talking about how you feed your mind or what you allow into your thoughts. Pure means *clean, perfect, not messed up*. Think about a new pair of tennis shoes. They are so clean and perfect the first time you wear them. Your mom probably tells you to stay on the sidewalk and out of the mud. Why?

We want to keep our thoughts and hearts pure like new tennis shoes. Once you accept Jesus as your Lord and Savior, you are made pure in His eyes. You are clean. But you need to avoid the "mud" like you do with your new shoes. You want to watch your step. This means to be careful with your choices. It means to be careful about what you listen to and what you watch. This will become more and more important as you get older.

Psalm 32:1
The Message

Count yourself lucky, how happy you must be—
you get a fresh start, your slate's wiped clean.

💬 Something to talk about:

Can you think of a time you made a good choice (and avoided *stepping in the mud*)?

✏️ Something to write about:

Write about when you asked Jesus into your heart.

_____

_____

_____

_____

_____

_____

_____

_____

_____

_____

☑️ Something to do:

Take a few minutes to thank Jesus for dying on the cross for you, for making you clean, and for making your heart pure.

DAY 5

Whatever is Lovely

Whatever is lovely, think about such things. I have seen some beautiful things in the world, and I bet you have too! It's easy to thank God for whatever is lovely when you see the snowcapped mountains, a colorful field of flowers, or an orange, red, and pink sunset.

Lovely means *beautiful*, but it is more than what we see with our eyes. Lovely also means beauty inside, beauty that comes from your heart. Showing kindness and encouraging others can show inner beauty or loveliness. It is important to say nice things to people and to look for the good in everyone and everything. Staying positive helps you look lovely from the inside out.

2 Thessalonians 3:13
NIV

And as for you, brothers and sisters, never tire of doing what is good.

💬 Something to talk about:

Can you think of a time you showed kindness to someone?

✏️ Something to write about:

Write about a time someone was kind to you and how it made you feel.

_____

_____

_____

_____

_____

_____

_____

_____

_____

_____

☑️ Something to do:

Say something positive and encouraging to someone in your family or to someone at school.

Whatever is Admirable

Whatever is admirable, think about such things. Hmm, this is a hard one. Admirable means to be held in great respect. You might have great respect for, or think highly of, a famous athlete or someone with a beautiful voice. You may admire a friend who makes good grades or who draws really well. These are all special gifts from God, and people work hard to develop these gifts. But more than that, it means you should have respect for God and His creation. This means showing respect to your parents, your family, your friends, and the earth.

God made beautiful things for us to admire, but most importantly, beautiful things are a reflection of His love for us.

Ephesians 5:21
The Message

Out of respect for Christ, be courteously reverent to one another.

💬 Something to talk about:

What have you seen in God's creation that is really cool, unusual, or beautiful?

✏️ Something to write about:

How can you show respect to your parents?

_____

_____

_____

_____

_____

_____

_____

_____

_____

_____

_____

☑️ Something to do:

Do something this week that shows respect to our earth.

DAY 7

Thanks

Being thankful is one way to have good thoughts. Look at these four different verses:

Psalm 107:1 (NCV) *Thank the Lord because He is good. His love continues forever.*
Psalm 118:1 (NCV) *Thank the Lord because He is good. His love continues forever.*
Psalm 118:29 (NCV) *Thank the Lord because He is good. His love continues forever.*
Psalm 136:1 (NCV) *Give thanks to the Lord because He is good. His love continues forever.*

Wow! All of these verses say we should give thanks to God because God is *good*! If you focus on God, then you are focusing on whatever is true, whatever is honorable, whatever is right, whatever is pure, whatever is lovely, whatever is admirable! You are thinking about what is good. You are filling your mind with God-thoughts.

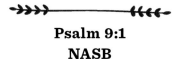

Psalm 9:1
NASB

I will give thanks to the Lord with all my heart; I will tell of all Your wonders.

💬 Something to talk about:

How can you remember to thank God every day?

✏️ Something to write about:

List three things you are thankful for.

_____

_____

_____

_____

_____

_____

_____

_____

_____

_____

_____

_____

_____

☑️ Something to do:

Tell three people why you are thankful for them.

DAY 8

Praise

Praising God is another way to show that you are thankful. Praise helps you focus on the good things God does. It is giving Him recognition. Praise is celebrating God and thanking Him for His love. You can also praise God by singing to Him. God is strong and mighty. There is nothing He cannot do. There are many verses in the book of Psalms about praising and thanking God. Most importantly, we want to acknowledge God for His goodness. Being thankful reminds us that God is good.

Psalm 100:4
NCV

Come into His city with songs of thanksgiving and
into His courtyards with songs of praise.
Thank Him and praise His name.

💬 Something to talk about:

How does God provide for you?

✏️ Something to write about:

List three things you can praise God for.

_____

_____

_____

_____

_____

_____

_____

_____

_____

☑️ Something to do:

Sing a praise song to God.

DAY 9

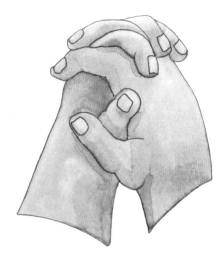

Prayer

Let's talk about prayer! Prayer is how you talk to God and how He talks to you. You can talk to Him just like you talk to your parents or your friends, *and* you can talk to Him anytime. Praying is one of the *most* important things you can do!

The Bible says God hears you when you pray. If it's important to you, it's important to God. He wants to hear what is on your mind. Talk to Him about your day. You can tell Him about things you hope to do tomorrow, or things you hope to do when you grow up. You don't have to use fancy words. Just talk normal!

1 Peter 3:12
ICB

The Lord sees the good people. He listens to their prayers.

💬 Something to talk about:

What is something you hope you can do as you get older? Play the guitar, build a house, sing on a stage, play baseball, have a family—tell God about it.

✏️ Something to write about:

Write down one thing you are going to pray about this week.

_____

_____

_____

_____

_____

_____

_____

_____

_____

_____

☑️ Something to do:

Set aside a time each day to be alone and pray. One sentence a day is a good way to start.

DAY 10

Prayer

Check out this Bible verse! In 1 Thessalonians 5:17, the Bible says, "Never stop praying" (ICB).

Well, that's easy! You can pray any time of day and in any location. When praying, you can thank God, worship God, and praise God. You can talk about your feelings or ask Him for help… anything! Anytime! Wow!

You can pray when you are happy and you can pray when you are sad. You can pray when you are confused. You can pray when you are mad. You can pray for your family and you can pray for your friends. Remember, it's just talking to God about what you are thinking.

Ephesians 6:18
NCV

Pray in the Spirit at all times with all kinds of prayers,
asking for everything you need. To do this you must always be ready
and never give up. Always pray for all God's people.

💬 Something to talk about:

Do you know that Jesus prayed? What do you think Jesus prayed about?

✏️ Something to write about:

Write something you want to tell God about.

_____

_____

_____

_____

_____

_____

_____

_____

_____

_____

☑️ Something to do:

Pick someone to pray for this week.

DAY 11

Prayer

I love the verse **James 5:16, "...When a believing person prays, great things happen."** God is leaning in and listening to you when you pray. You can give Him your worries. You can give Him your fears. The Bible tells you not to be afraid. In fact, the Bible says it 365 times! You can ask for help when things are hard. But most importantly, you can pray all kinds of prayers, all the time, asking for everything you need.

Philippians 4:6
ICB

Do not worry about anything. But pray and ask God for everything you need. And when you pray, always give thanks.

💬 Something to talk about:

Think about one of your favorite Bible characters. Was there a time he or she might have been afraid or worried?

✏️ Something to write about:

Write down something you are worried about or afraid of.

_____

_____

_____

_____

_____

_____

_____

_____

_____

_____

_____

☑ Something to do:

Ask God to help you be brave and confident.

DAY 12

Prayer

God speaks to us when we pray. Sometimes He helps us understand something better and sometimes He gives us a good idea. He also reminds us how much He loves us. His words to us can help us be strong and courageous. Find a place in your house where you can have some quiet time each day. This is a time to talk to God *and* to listen to Him.

I love Jeremiah 33:3. I want to pray and talk to God because He promises to tell me great and wonderful things. He promises to tell me things I cannot learn or know by myself. If I am not praying, I am missing out! I won't hear the special things that God wants to say to me. I believe He has personal things to tell you, too. I don't want you to miss out on the marvelous and wonderful things God wants to say to you.

Jeremiah 33:3
NASB

Call to Me and I will answer you, and I will tell you great
and mighty things, which you do not know.

💬 Something to talk about:

Talk to an adult about where you can go in your house to have a quiet time, a time to talk and listen to God.

✏️ Something to write about:

Have you ever had a great idea just pop into your head? It might have been an idea of something to make or do. It might have been about a kind way to help someone. What was that idea?

_____

_____

_____

_____

_____

_____

_____

_____

_____

_____

_____

☑️ Something to do:

Pay attention to your thoughts. When you have a good idea or a good thought about something, be sure and thank God for talking to you.

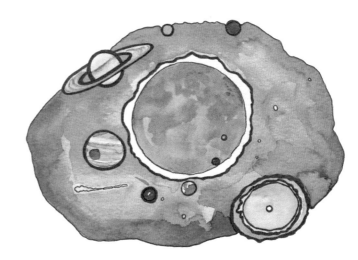

DAY 13

Prayer

Gerald loves it when we pray. He loves that we believe in Him. He wants us to pray with confidence. After all, He created the entire universe and everything in it! He can do anything!

When we pray and talk to God, He wants us to pray boldly, believing that He will listen and respond. But remember, we have to listen back.

Your parents might be praying about an important job coming up or a decision they need to make. Is there something on your mind that seems overwhelming, something you might be worried or confused about? Maybe you know someone who is sad or lonely, maybe you have an injury, or maybe you know someone who needs to hear about Jesus. You can pray about something big or something small. You can pray about something going on right now or something that might happen later. But remember, pray boldly and with confidence.

James 1:6
NCV

But when you ask God, you must believe and not doubt.

💬 Something to talk about:

Think about what you've learned over the last few days about prayer. Why is it important to pray about everything?

✏️ Something to write about:

What do you want to pray about?

_____

_____

_____

_____

_____

_____

_____

_____

_____

_____

☑️ Something to do:

It's fun to write down your prayers. Put the date on the paper. Then sit back and watch God work!

DAY 14

friends

Friends

Let's talk about friends. The Bible has many stories about friends. Moses and Aaron led their people out of slavery. Their story is one of support and strength. David and Jonathan were unlikely friends. Their story is one of honesty and loyalty. The friendship between Ruth and Naomi began because Naomi suffered great loss. Their story is one of faithfulness and security. Paul and Timothy were friends who shared the gospel together. Their story is one of trust and respect.

The greatest friendship of all is between you and Jesus. Before you were born, He knew you and loved you. His compassion for you is beyond measure. He came to save you. He died for you. This is something you already know and believe. Because He loved you that much, you can *choose* to live with hope and joy.

John 15:23
NASB

Greater love has no one than this, that one lay down his life for his friends.

💬 Something to talk about:

What makes a good friend?

✏️ Something to write about:

Write a thank you note to Jesus for being such a good friend.

_____

_____

_____

_____

_____

_____

_____

_____

_____

_____

☑️ Something to do:

Do something kind for one of your friends.

DAY 15

Friends

It's important to understand that who we hang around affects who we are. I Corinthians 15:33 says, "Do not be fooled: 'Bad friends ruin good habits'" (ICB).

God wants us to have good relationships with people. Friends offer love, encouragement, fun, and support. Jesus spent a lot of time with His friends. He went fishing with them. He spent the night at their house. He had meals with them. He prayed with them. He chose His friends very carefully, and so should you. Right now, you are probably friends with your cousins or with the children of your parents' friends. As you get older, you will begin to choose friends your parents may not know. It's so important to choose your friends wisely.

Proverbs 22:24
ICB

Don't make friends with someone who easily gets angry.
Don't spend time with someone who has a bad temper.

💬 Something to talk about:

Why is it important to have good, kind friends?

✏️ Something to write about:

What will you look for in a friend?

_____

_____

_____

_____

_____

_____

_____

_____

_____

☑️ Something to do:

Look for children at school or church who don't seem to have many friends. Include them in a game or ask them to sit with you.

DAY 16

Friends

In order to have good friends, you have to *be* a good friend. Sometimes you form friendships with people in your family like Ruth and Naomi did. Moses and Aaron were brothers and also friends. They used their strengths and talents to help each other. Sometimes friendships form instantly, even though you are from very different backgrounds, like David and Jonathan. One was a prince and one was a shepherd. Sometimes friends travel like Paul and Timothy because they have the same goal or mission. Bottom line, friends are willing to sacrifice or give up what they want in order to help each other. Friendships are one of God's many blessings.

You can pray about the friends you have right now. You can pray about the friends you will have when you are older. I encourage you to choose friends who love Jesus. Surround yourself with kind people who choose to do what is right.

Proverbs 17:17
ICB

A friend loves at all times. A brother is always there to help you.

💬 Something to talk about:

What do you have in common with your friends? How are you alike? How are you different?

✏️ Something to write about:

How can you be a good friend to others?

_____

_____

_____

_____

_____

_____

_____

☑️ Something to do:

Ask God to help you pick your friends wisely.

DAY 17

The Bible

The Bible is full of promises and hope for those who love God. Just as it is important to pray, it is also important to read the Bible. God talks to us through prayer, but He also talks to us through His Word. We can find wisdom and truth in God's Word. There are a lot of things in the Bible that are hard to understand, but there are so many things we *can* understand. The important thing is to put forth effort and spend time with God. He just wants to hang out with us!

You have already found a special spot in your house to pray. Now find a quiet place to read the Bible. It may be the same place. I know schedules are busy, but I believe our days will be better when we spend time with God. I like to have breakfast with Jesus, so I try to read and pray in the mornings. But remember, we can pray anytime, all day long!

2 Timothy 3:16-17
NIV

All scripture is God-breathed and is useful for teaching, rebuking, correction and training in righteousness, so that the servant of God may be thoroughly equipped for every good work.

💬 Something to talk about:

Where will you add reading the Bible to your schedule?

✏️ Something to write about:

Why do you think it is important to read the Bible?

_____

_____

_____

_____

_____

_____

_____

_____

_____

☑️ Something to do:

Sometimes it is fun to read your Bible with a friend, a sibling, or a parent. Try it this week then talk about what you read.

The Bible

I love to read. Reading may not be your favorite thing right now, but I believe you love a good story. The Bible is full of good stories. There are sword fights and battles. There are kings and queens. There is a great flood, a river turned to blood, and the parting of a sea! There is music and dancing. There is friendship and love. These action-packed stories teach us about God's love and faithfulness. These stories remind us that God is trustworthy. These stories give us the courage to do hard things. We see how strongly God loves His people. I am glad we are His people!

Exodus 34:6
NCV

The Lord passed in front of Moses and said, "I am the Lord. The Lord is a God who shows mercy, who is kind, who doesn't become angry quickly, who has great love and faithfulness."

💬 Something to talk about:

Why do you think the Bible is full of stories about people like you and me?

✏️ Something to write about:

What is your favorite Bible story? Can you write about it or draw a picture?

_____

_____

_____

_____

_____

_____

_____

_____

_____

_____

_____

☑️ Something to do:

Retell your favorite Bible story to a friend this week.

DAY 19

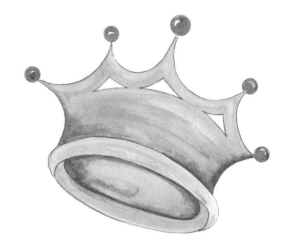

The Bible

Sometimes we think that the Bible stories happened so long ago that they don't affect us, but there is something for us to learn from every story. Some stories are about people who doubted God and how He showed His faithfulness. Think about the Israelites as Moses led them to the promised land. Some stories are about people who obeyed God, like Esther and Noah. These stories show how God blessed them for their obedience. I love the verse in Esther's story that says, "...you may have been chosen queen for just such a time as this." And if you know, or remember, because she obeyed God, her people were saved from death! The same is true of Noah. His obedience saved his family. The Bible is full of stories that can inspire us.

Psalm 128:1
ICB

Happy are those who respect the Lord and obey Him.

🗨 Something to talk about:

Many stories talk about obedience. Why do you think obedience is important?

✏ Something to write about:

What is something you learned from your favorite Bible story?

_____

_____

_____

_____

_____

_____

_____

_____

☑ Something to do:

Memorize today's Bible verse.

DAY 20

The Promises

The Bible not only gives us instructions for how to live, but it is also full of promises from God. Exodus says the Lord will fight for us. In Deuteronomy, the Bible declares God will never leave us. Isaiah states that God gives us strength. Jeremiah says the Lord gives us hope and a future. In James, the Bible says God will give us wisdom. First John says He will forgive us of our sins. There are so many promises about how much God loves us and cares for us. No wonder Philippians 4:6 tells us not to be anxious about anything.

God gives us promises. It is our job to listen to Him and to obey His commands. I know you know about the Ten Commandments, but I especially love the verse below. It reminds us of the first commandment to come with a promise.

Ephesians 6:1-3
NCV

Children, obey your parents as the Lord wants, because it is the right thing to do. The command says, "Honor your father and mother." This is the first command with a promise with it —"Then everything will be well with you, and you will have a long life on earth."

So, read your Bible, spend time in prayer, obey God's commandments, obey your parents, and look for the best in the beautiful life God has given you!

Amen

AUTHOR'S NOTE

There is definitely a unique joy in becoming a grandparent. Suddenly, the world is wide open with new possibilities. There are new adventures dancing around every corner and opportunities waiting to be seized. Once the grandchildren began arriving, I knew my responsibility and desire was to pray for them every day, and their salvation was my foremost prayer. When the eldest two asked Jesus into their hearts, I found that I had so much to tell them. This 20-day devotional began as a way to share my heart and experiences with them.

AUTHOR'S THANKS

Thank you, friends and family, for cheering me on.
You are my biggest fans, and I will be forever grateful!

Thank you, Dr. Joe Paris, for your support with research and consultation.

Made in the USA
Monee, IL
26 July 2022

10389865R00031